THE BABIES

Sabrina Orah Mark

Winner of the Saturnalia Books Poetry Prize 2004
Selected by Jane Miller

saturnalia books

THE BABIES

Sabrina Orah Mark

Saturnalia Books
7600 Cherokee Street
2nd Floor
Philadelphia, PA 19118
info @ www.saturnaliabooks.com

ISBN 0-9754990-1-7

Book Design by Saturnalia Books

Cover Art: Walter Rothschild, The Avifauna of Laysan and the neighbouring islands with a complete history to date of the birds of the Hawaiian possession (London: R.H. Porter, 1893-1900). © Smithsonian Institute

Author Photograph: Ari Mark

Distributed by:
Small Press Distribution
1341 Seventh Street
Berkeley, CA 94710-1409
1-800-869-7553

Grateful acknowledgement to the editors of the following publications in which these poems first appeared, and to the organizations which supported me while I wrote them: *American Letters & Commentary*, *American Poet*, *Barrow Street*, *The Bitter Oleander*, *The Canary*, *Conduit*, *Denver Quarterly*, *Gulf Coast*, *Fence*, *The Indiana Review*, *Northwest Review* and *Volt*.

Thanks to the Fine Arts Work Center in Provincetown and the Glenn Schaeffer Fellowship for their generous support.

Thanks to my teachers and friends for their limitless insight and encouragement, especially Claudia Rankine for being there from the beginning; to Oni Buchanan, Joshua Crane, Michael Dumanis, Tim Earley, Jane Elias, Lara Glenum, Thomas Heise, Matthew Shindell, and John Woods, for endlessly supporting this project; to Joanna Goodman, Henry Israeli, and Jane Miller, my total gratitude. Finally, I could not have completed the project without the support and love of my family.

"A Kaddish" is in memory of my grandfather, Eugene Mark.

Einmal, der Tod hatte Zulauf,
verbargst du dich in mir.

Once, when death was mobbed,
you took shelter in me.

—Paul Celan

CONTENTS

FOUR

THE WALTER B. INTERVIEWS

SIX

for my brothers, Ari and Etan

The world is, in spite of everything, very over. I asked the carnie, and he said *Marvin*. And I said yes? And he said *Marvin, it's very over*. I nodded in agreement, as I rearranged the wisteria. Also, the day was clear. A single silk stocking hung in the air. And the carnie, his hands in his pockets, said Marvin. And I said yes? And he looked at me tenderly and said *the dish has run away from the spoon*. And I said *yes, it was bound to happen*. That night, in his orange pickup truck, we made love for the last time, as it sunk into a muddy swamp. Somewhere else, a tree was burning.

ONE

Amen

Whether or not it was the trumpeter, or the brass, or the brass against a certain naked foot. Whether or not you are what's left to be solved of the drowned, I rented a room beside the Butcher's Lake. Mostly sadness. They'd come around at night and ask me questions. From far off, we could hear bathtubs or radios or chandeliers being thrown out of windows. "Heads or tails," they'd ask. "As a friend," I'd say, "I recommend the head." They never asked me if I knew you, although I wish they had. It was a mild winter to be deserted and the black sailboats seemed tired and a little old. I kept sparrows loose in the kitchen, which aroused their curiosity as they fingered my scars. One day, they kneeled inside me and called me a Jew. At first I rejected their offer, but they were right and promised me a lady's hat. I did not fear them until I wanted to be afraid. The lake was guarded and the road to town was closed.

THE DUMB SHOW

Because the gods believe they ought, like buried corsets, to make the best of a bad bargain, they have begun to show their flesh a little;

their black hair expanding into heaven knows what…the muddy scratch of stick figures in the dark, the ones who have begun to delicately call themselves Madeleine rub their sleepy eye from behind that blue monocle, and the others with a futurist thirst for tin, crimson curtain lowering on the last act, I assure you: there was no beginning,

as in: *before he even made his entrance*…The whole place was in an uproar. And after? And before? I went back behind the curtain and returned in a woman's blouse, battle-weary…The men above me were shouting. The women above me were shouting. The electric lights went out as arranged. I felt on the ground for the black wig, though it was not clear whose was whose. I caressed the bone-hard surface of a stranger's chest until he pulled me to his lap and brought my fingers to his mouth.

THE SONG

The milk is mildly foxed. The sky, too, is mildly foxed.
And it is wonderful to see the dexterity with which the
dark beak hangs on, although it too, is mildly foxed. As
are the woods. As is the fox. We are all mildly foxed.
Even Mama. Even Mama is mildly foxed.

When Mama fell in love with the ornithologist she
began to sneak from the house at night and return with
her pockets full of water lettuce, feathers, bits of nest.
She began to save electricity. She began to like certain
people. The ornithologist, according to the papers,
spoke in a mischievous language and had a beard. The
ornithologist, according to Mama, knew exactly how he
made her feel. "Like a mildly foxed apricot!" she would
say, swinging me around by the hips. She would hold me
up to the light. She would kiss me on the neck. She
would put me down. Over and over again. For hours. It
is true that jealousy is what brought me to spy on Mama
that night. I too wanted to feel like a mildly foxed
apricot. I too wanted to like certain people. It was
February. I wore a blouse with large red pockets.
Although Mama had already lost me as a mother, what
happened is still difficult to say. I saw Mama. I saw the
ornithologist. I followed them to the green balcony

where he cut for her a loaf of bread with a large pair of
scissors. I could hear through his mischievous language.
He had a plan. To get rid of the birds, he said. All the
mildly foxed birds. He called it *end low song*. He sang
it softly.

THANK YOU

In the burnt attic we are all a little dead. Bewilder
shouting about her nightgown, and through the window
you can see the rest of us walking around with our shoes
and stockings in our hands. But as the story goes, it was
time to write a thank you note:

> *Thank you for the wedding glove. We split it seven
> ways. When we looked inside first it was cold second
> it sent shivers down our heart. Bones got caught in
> the fence. Thank you for the way the ribbons went.
> Bewilder's all choked up.*

BOX THREE, SPOOL FIVE

I have a little accordion. I wrap it in brown paper. Tonight I take it out to the porch and miss you, one word at a time. *Lustspiel*, I slowly mouth into the dark blue night. Behind me I can hear me shuffling closer and closer: *Be again. Be. Again.* I try very hard to pray with all these hands against my back. I miss the keeper of this accordion. I miss the fairgrounds. But most of all I miss you playing in the five-cent booth. And I in my wire gown. And you in your wire gown. Tonight I unwrap the accordion and your white hair spills out. Tonight even you cannot take the place of you. I peel your birthmark from my cheek and toss it to the yard crows. For you to feel their beak marks would be everything.

TWO

In The Origami Fields

where I fold and unfold my left arm into November, my hair
        into my sister,
where the black-gloved woman plays my heart like a crumpled
        violin,
where I stand creased and lusting for paper, where I have no
        more dead lovers
than you, where beautiful girls are always asked for directions,
where I keep myself real, flirting with the ventriloquists,
where my father holds me like a paper doll, where doors can be
        torn down
swiftly, where neither one of us is a miracle,

I understand only this:

It is lonely in a place that can burn so fast.

THE BABIES

Some thought it was because of all the babies I suddenly seemed to be having. Others, that I should pay for the damages. Fact is, I wasn't getting any older, so I bought a small aquarium, and skipped town. Took up with a toy store owner until he left me for a more beautiful robot. Took up with a reader of instructional booklets. Never mind. I was lost. By the time I arrived at Mrs. Greenaway's, it was clear I was nowhere at all. In exchange for room and board, I'd rearrange her furniture, her birthmarks, her quiet animals, until they took on more satisfying shapes. Sometimes the shapes were simple, like a mustache or a pipe. Sometimes they were more complicated arrangements, like the one of dead Mr. Greenaway's closed barbershop. Over the years, as Mrs. Greenaway and I became more and more vague, the shapes did too. For identification purposes, we'd give them names like *She Wasn't Fooling Anyone, She Was Hurt and She Was Hurt Bad or The Insides of Doctors*. One night when I was working on a piece I thought I'd call Symphony, Symphony, the shapes began to slip out of my hands. At first, as Mrs. Greenaway remembers, the sound of broken glass. Then the trumpets. Then the terrible music of all those babies I once seemed to be suddenly having, marching, like soldiers, in rows. Then their round wet bellies coming towards me. Mrs. Greenaway still talks about how expertly they gathered me into their tiny arms. And how they took me away not like a prisoner. But like a mother. Into a past I still swear I never had.

Hello

I am one anatomy and take turns. Sometimes after dinner I wrap them up in newspaper. Before they grow cold or one is still sleeping. Hello. They call me Zillah. I fell in love on the night train to Warsaw. Every human situation strikes me as a terrific joke. I am a torn off blouse in that red river. Ha ha holocaust. I can't complain. There are rules and there are onions and there are beautiful outer skins. Is that you, little darling? Let me see your visitor's pass. Some workmen from the gravel pit found Zillah holding an open umbrella, waving goodbye to her fans and singing "she fell in love on the night train to Warsaw." Hello. They call me Zillah. I touch them as they try to climb the wall. Let us tell you what it's like to be Zillah, they say, as they part my wig down the middle. It's like

THE NECKLACE

I feel the hummingbirds around my neck on the condition that the others do not profit from my bone-collared dress She is well aware that the only way to remain desired is to postpone the hummingbirds. She is reduced to an instrument. What we encounter here is the basic neurotic strategy of falling down the stairs. I smile like a botched angel to prevent the other's jouissance. Here are my wings all choked up. Here is my symptom. Here is my dream, my strangle, my slip of the tongue. She will talk continuously to take away the empty in which the underlying conflict might emerge. I am scared about my necklace. She is obsessed with the notion that the little birds were taken from her. They were my little birds, humming. Not theirs. She is so radically unconscious she may never be remembered. My little humming birds, not theirs.

HEIMLICHKEITEN

I

One green flower pasted to a burnt up overcoat
mysteries the mottled gowns hung from the shower rod,
freaks the daffodilies out, *lucky girls get in the house*. Easy
to lose time, I gather my dolls, stare at my hands as you
rake the thistledown like such silk, and by color I
assemble them so that Bones will be the last one in, most
beautiful in her cut out curtains, and underneath she
is talking.

II

No playing "brides" in the house, only in the yard.
If Everyone removes her redskin dress she will ruin it
for the others, and then what? *Sit in the corner so that
everything is touching*. One day we will be less
mechanical and leave you.

III

We marionette. We only story. We terrible to soil, and
come gather. We trouble up the yard, *what's a mother?
how much longer?*

THREE

BLACK MARKET

What else could I have done, but check into the
Massacre Motel. Cheat the rubble collector out of old
rage and oranges. Her last glass bracelet. As in the story
that begins *what is her name—and ends she doesn't know,*
she doesn't know. Call me Berlin. Call me Your Last
Descension. I've been watching you for a long time
stunned by the restlessness of the black market.
Everything turning into something else. The soldier's
gold teeth slipping into your hands like wedding rings.
Then slipping away. Even forgiveness, as I watch you
trade our mattress for a miniature boxcar. Even its
wheels turn. Because in this story there is no little girl
in the rocks whispering to her dog *forever, forever*.
Even she wants sugar bread. Even she is dying for a
gamble. Tomorrow her dog will wake up locked in a
stranger's trunk for a good laugh. I want to point its fear
at you or, worse, among the devastated walls of this
cheap metropolis, barter away everything you've ever
called me: burnt string, broken ladder, violent one, until
I am unrecognizable. Even to myself.

Osip Zoo

There are those for whom Osip Zoo does not exist, and then there are the rest of us. With our cages, and trumpets, and string. We look to Osip Zoo for the rules, and march unafraid to the laboratory. We hold our children in our mouths. Sleep, He says, among piles of red stoves. And it is there we sleep. Lift your nightgown for seven days at the entrance of The Black Tent. And for seven days we lift.

THE MUSTACHE

Everything about the young foreign taxidermist was
overdone. Did he absolutely have to wear the apron with
the tiny red castles in the shop? Or weave, at night, in
and out of the trees? I don't think so. I would bring him
buckets of ice water day after day hoping he would just
cool off a bit. Fact is, he never did. But to be fair, he
really was practicing what the papers called, "heroic
medicine." It was love. I admit it. It was *fancy* love. I was
the envy of the world, being hitched up with such a
genius, and that felt good. Of course, these days, I can't
touch rope or a small child without thinking of him.
Without expecting his large hands to come out of
nowhere. We were, as mother said, both "slowly losing
our minds." He'd talk for hours about hygiene, the Water
Cure for example, and wrote an award-winning essay on
the Electric Bath as a way to treat hysteria in the female
fox. "Too many foxes," he would say, shaking his fist, "too
many foxes running around like chickens with their
heads cut off." In the winter months we would ride our
bicycles down to the scrap- metal yard where he would
make love to me in devout silence. The delight in his
eyes when he found that small cage! He was both tender
and rough, and I had never, and will never again, be as
touched by another man. I didn't notice the black

mustache growing slowly but unmercifully on his left shoulder until two or three years into the affair. At first it seemed harmless. A small patch of dead grass. But eventually I couldn't help but only see the large dark field. Its silent twitching. By then it was already early fall, and the fact is, it tore us apart.

THE VISIT

At 103 South Governor Street, Apartment One, I visit Old Gerta. She is bent over a mandolin. Her father, half god, half kitsch, is rummaging through her new white purse in the parlor. "By next Tuesday," he mumbles sweetly, "she'll be dead." Gerta looks up and winks. "Had I been a poet," she says, "there would have been a lake." I unbutton my blouse, and Gerta creeps into my lap. A cold key is pressed into my hand. There is the sound of shoveling in the yard. "I've missed you terribly," I sigh, disguising my voice. Her father is floating between us, and I climb onto his shoulders to get a better look. Old Gerta is as lovely as she was in that storm. Old Gerta, Old Gerta… "Unlock my father and bring me my story," she says. I am rising on my knees. I am reaching in. It has bits of bone sticking to it, and blood, and it smells like my breath once did against Gerta's red skirt. I am scared of its closeness. I am scared of Gerta burying her head in my thighs like a ghost. There is a knock at the door. I need a drink. I am certain it is you.

THE PROPOSAL

Vintage darkling, metropolis? I asked. But you said no
without sugar, you said arms. I said please. I was bent
at the knee and scripting. You said *fix it*. Sky
turning from broomstick to bone, you said angel, I said yes,
quiet as a hill going up, I said *yes*. A hunger. Or to get to
           the bottom
of it, *I said plate of oranges with pepper on top*, you said
nothing. I said rustle, with a bad case of Doll's Eye, I said—

rustle,

you said nothing. I dusted it off. I was glad to be inside it for
           a while,

you said *stop*, you said *dandelion more*. I spun around, *a corset
throat farewell*, I asked, *a latch?*

Non Vixit

Late one night I enter the laboratory. There is only one animal. There is less of it now and more of other animals, but there is only one animal. Something is waiting for me inside this experiment. I want for it a language. I want for it a little evidence. There is only one animal. I study it from far behind the magnifying glass. It is biting on a Z with many zeroes after it. There is less of it now and more of other animals, but there is only one animal. Ladders we carry to see how far the ladder takes us. Machines we build to feel the sadness of machines. When I pull the cord there is only one animal. Do not be afraid, you are its world.

FOUR

The Experiments Lasted Through The Winter

We asked, what is this? It rustled. We dug a hole. What is
this, we asked, a nocturama? No, we agreed, the thing was
not a nocturama. A nocturama is when you cannot catch
their breath. We nodded. We dug a hole. Our white hair
warmed around the thing, we asked, is this a genesis? No, we
agreed, the thing was not a genesis. A genesis is when he
sweeps across the water. We nodded. It rustled. We stood
closer to each other, we asked, what is this, a stillness? We
watched it from a distance, we agreed, the thing was not a
stillness. A stillness is when their legs come close. We dug a
hole. We climbed the tree to watch it from below. What is
this, we asked, to look at the boy? We touched our
instruments and agreed the thing was not to look at the boy.
To look at the boy is when there is no boy. We dug a hole.
We weakened. We could no longer touch the thing.
The thing, we were afraid, had lied to us. What is this, we
asked, a father? We dug a hole. No, we agreed, the thing was
not a father. A father is when you raise the cloth to his lips.
What is this, we asked, we leaned against each other, what is
this, a war? No, we agreed, the thing was not a war. A war is
when you cannot hear the animals.

THE ROBOT

At the spectacle, I win a little robot and strap it to my thigh. At the spectacle, my arm keeps popping up. *Zwang!* I cough, distantly. By dawn they arrive on one leg making promises. I help them pull your plastic hips from the long dark cord. I tell them your secrets. They dress me in your wet clothes and drag me softly past the fuhrer's beautiful hands. "For twenty-five cents," they say, "you can touch them." The robot drifts off to sleep. I look around as if remembering. I look around for loose change. My arm pops up. The robot is startled awake. It opens its aluminum eyes. I feed it hearts of palm and my arm.... "You are lonely," they say, burying what is left of your hips in my hair. The robot moans bashfully. I moan too. But the robot moans louder, its black bangs already growing over its eyes.

THE EGGS

We are combing the baby for fish and I say Asa, Asa, there is no baby, there are no fish, and she says yes and this goes on for some time. Afterwards, we watch the laboratory lights, in the distance, blink. When I think of all the years Asa and I have spent together I want to pick up the baby and go out the back gate. No baby. No gate. I wasn't expecting this, Asa. Your hair is the color of baby, Asa. No baby. No hair. The mud on your blouse, Asa, unbutton your blouse. When the others arrive I point at Asa and say there is no mud, no blouse, and the others laugh, and I feel strange, and this goes on for some time. Afterwards, Asa and I drive to the parking lot and take photographs of the thick birds dragging their eggs across the asphalt. No Asa. No asphalt. I touch Asa's glove and ask, then to whom am I speaking, Asa? And Asa says to the eggs, Asa, you are always speaking to the eggs. And I say yes, and this goes on for some time.

The Fever

"Love is like a soufflé," I sang as I skipped into glass. It's sheer porn to sit by the oven and chew on the fingernails. With needle and thread I'll mother a Jew. Such spangle it hurts. Such bedroom eyes. A hatch of lovers and no sign of the Monday Boy; am I too ordinary, tell me, thy name. I am as among the cat's red tongue as I'll ever be. Could I live my whole life on kitchen, in air? Would it be unwieldy? Would the neighbors talk outside the jail? I care not a toe, but a fever. There's no end to the way the emergency exit will smile. Voluptuously and in a clorox panic, I've drawn back my skin with this crayon.

THE ETERNAL FOOTMEN

On the fifth night, they return with news from the front. They smell of sawdust, and it makes me blush. I recognize them from the picture books. From the opera in the woods. "It's time for bed," I say, and they tuck me in. One hands me fish wrapped in *The Candelabra Papers*. Another hisses *disco* in my ear. "Sweet dreams," I reply. Like six million little thieves, I ask them to stay. I give them my curtains. I ask for my brother. They hand me a red scarf.

.

Zero Visibility

(Applause)

except for the bridge that is lost in our car, we are good
drivers because crash is delicate, because direction is
slippery, we look both ways, *oh inspector——it's happening
again*. You said – left. And we merged. You said – leaving
and the interstate got sneaky. We curve like the
mechanical limbs of little girls tucked inside a peep box.
Our tops are down. It's a stop sign, and it's hilarious—
it's *an intersection——oh ma-ma, oh inspector*, it's a very icy
day! Looking good. Looking good.

(Privately)

we took the car as far as you took us. A city will, yes,
will stop like that will—*yes ma-ma who is not ma-ma*,
a sign will appear up ahead. A man will appear up ahead.
He is holding a box he cannot remember or he is holding
a box. Our tongues are dusty. We drive diagonal on
the sidewalk.

(To repeatedly fail)

to follow instructions is to want the box back. We are
good drivers, *because loss is windy* ("and each knowing
the other was going to die"), a bird will stand in the
middle of the road and place its wings down.

Isn't that a love?

As if we recalled one word that made us forget
everything. *Oh inspector, isn't that a steer?*

THE WALTER B. INTERVIEWS

{ I }

You once said that when you scratched at the mole on Walter B.'s neck you could hear the Goat Song. What did you mean by that?

I meant that the meats must first be boiled, and then sliced. That's all I meant.

Can you describe for me your years with Walter B.?

I used the rake to take care of most of it. Walter B. provided me with enough index cards to account for the rest. At night we would lean against the stove, and in the morning, when the collector arrived, we would go with him.

According to Walter B.'s last notes, "form mimics disease." What did he mean by that?

Since Walter B.'s disgrace it has become impossible for me to say how certain things happen.

Did Walter B. keep any animals?

He destroyed them all to save himself the disappointment. Though, you must understand, I continued to love Walter B. despite this, as one loves a child who has taken the place of another.

In "The New Pastoral" Walter B.'s mama writes: "I amused myself with his head / in the Hat District —

If not for Walter B.'s mama, the final assemblage could have been easily avoided.

Can you describe for me the final assemblage?

It was almost daybreak. A small piece of muscle fell from Walter B.'s mouth. This was the first real news of extinction. At first, I tried not to look at it, or think about its sadness. It was the collector, at the end, who buried it in the dirt with the others. Even then I knew, as you know now, it would return, like Walter B. would return, over and over again…I wanted to lie down next to it and wait for its soft directions…

But you were afraid?

I was afraid. This was the very beginning, as I said, of the extinction. A woman couldn't lie down next to a small piece of muscle without knowing she had at that very moment risked everything. This might seem difficult to believe, but I was such a human being once. I had a kind of feeling living among Walter B.

Can you sing for me a little of the Goat Song?

Zugzwang, zugzwang, zugzwang…

{ II }

Walter B. writes, "Nullpunkt, nullpunkt. Redemption through labor." How long did you live this way?

I lived this way until the first real news of the extinction.

Can you describe for me The Gesundheithaus?

From where I was sitting, if I moved my head two inches to either side, I could see the babies. Had they just once gathered around me, as they gathered around Walter B. night after night, like teeth...

Why did the babies not gather around you?

I called them Baba, which means, in the winter, "an action or an instance of negligence."

And in the summer?

"My little white suitcase."

Was there ever any evidence?

There was never any evidence, but there was always his hat on the table. Each time there was something different inside. Walter

B. would ask, "What do you see?" And in my most water-damaged accent I'd say "human" or "hair," but never the truth.

Were there others?

In examining every bit of documentation concerning the others, it is clear that there was no other.

In "The New Pastoral" Walter B.'s mama writes, "he walks / through the goat / like a terrible machine."

Yes. He walked through the goat like a terrible machine.

The last photographs show Walter B. going slowly through The Gesundheithaus. He barely recognizes you. Can you describe for me what, in these last photographs, you were feeling?

It is a feeling like what, at the end, had happened to the babies.

{ III }

Can you describe for me Walter B. after the desertion?

Too much architecture, not enough rain.

How do you recognize Walter B. in their abandoned homes?

He is the only one, among drifts of white hair, who knows several things at once.

Why, at the end of the Goat Song, does Walter B. stop feeding the babies?

At the end of the Goat Song, it becomes impossible to grow this old.

In "The New Pastoral," Walter B.'s mama writes, "for Walter B. / I scatter / like meats."

As you might have expected, when the collector arrived to measure Walter B.'s mama for The Exhibition, she confessed to no such scatter.

Can you describe for me The Exhibition?

Like the bulbs, we were dipped into milk and hung. We swayed and we shed, gently. Later that evening the collector led us into the undressing room where, to the others' delight, I posed like a small piece of muscle.

In an entry dated after The Exhibition, Walter B. writes: "When I saw her in the undressing room I was no longer the same. I was no longer myself. Each time I see her, there are fewer and fewer instructions."

When Walter B. for the first time saw me, he called me Beatrice. Should I ever, he explained, need to become Beatrice one day.

Have you ever?

Once in his arms, and once behind the wire.

Sometimes, Beatrice, someone is assigned when   there is no
one else. It is too late for you, Beatrice,   and it is too late
for you to dig for me up their fresh hooves, their fresh hooves, in
your terrible smock. Even among the Brusselalia, you remain
ungathered. Oh my Beatrice, my darling, it was you   who was
the first real news of the extinction, and it was you who I destroyed
first   to save myself the disappointment. Runaway   like a
hoop, or I will paint on your knees, Beatrice,   or I will lead you
to the basin for the last time so as not   to disturb me, Beatrice,
       go in further than usual. You have allowed each hoof to
freely handle you. You have interrupted the babies,   Beatrice,
with your profound need for a sense   of well being. You
are a Beatrice bent over a smaller Beatrice   bent over a
clock that goes *trice, trice, trice.* There is nothing   left for
you inside me   to hatch. Tell me a real story that
begins   *Beatrice was a criminal* and only then will I slap my
hand away   among you. For what is a crime, my Beatrice,
       if it is not what you do beside me. What is a crime
if it is not done miserably behind the Beatrice Coffin. Walk
with me,   Beatrice, behind the Beatrice Coffin.   Grow
your hair, Beatrice, so I can comb   it.

The Interview

{ IV }

When Walter B. said of you "vulnerable" what did he mean by that?

He meant vulgar, vulture. He meant I came to him vaguely in the vestibule. When Walter B. said of me "vulnerable," he meant very, very. He meant what I saw with the vision cloth. He meant vast.

When Walter B. said of you "vulnerable" what did he mean by that?

I wanted to carry his parcels for a long time.

When Walter B. said of you "vulnerable" what did he mean by that?

You must understand that by this time Walter B. had sunk into what the doctors called "a patriotic grief." Every day, like a dead soldier, he would go to the refreshment room, bundled in opossum, and do nothing but dread his dear, dear country. He began to speak too much of the collector. When Walter B. said of me "vulnerable" he may have said lean, or rubble, or bare. He may have said near.

When Walter B. said of you "vulnerable" what did he mean by that?

I did to Walter B. an awful thing. For him, I blushed.

When Walter B. said of you "vulnerable" what did he mean by that?

I remember now why nothing was more satisfying to Walter B. than how I always kept, on our walks, half-a-step behind him. In those days, I often felt in advance of the feeling.

When Walter B. said of you vulnerable what did he mean by that?

One day I will tell you about our living room.

When Walter B. said of you "vulnerable" what did he mean by that?

Zwangzug, zwangzug, zwangzug...

The Interview

{ V }

Nothing, according to Walter B., is ever lost inside a zoo. Can you elaborate?

Lately I have been thinking about discretion.

Would you prefer not to have been involved at all?

In "The New Pastoral", Walter B.'s mama did write, "…I prefer / she had not been / involved / at all…"

According to the early drafts, "The New Pastoral" originally was called "The Human Comedy." When did it change?

Walter B. said, "turn around." He brushed the babies' damp gray hair against my neck.

Would you read for me aloud that sign above Walter B.'s head?

It must be cold under all those lights.

How do you feel?

I feel a little bored.

Like a zoo?

Yes, like a zoo.

In that case, would you like to hear a joke?

If you can remember...

How many marks did Walter B.'s hollow cost?

I've heard this one before. It cost only one.

THE INTERVIEW

{ VI }

Did it look like a completely strange world? Another world, I mean.

It was not a world.

According to "The Ledger," Z is "Them; Beauty." Can you elaborate?

It was not a world.

And "T" is what "Consolidation?" What "Experiment; Lasted?"

It was not a world. They introduced themselves as "Walter B." and "The Collector." I did not belong there.

If it was not a world then how do you explain the basin? How do you explain the suitcase, the babies, their entrance? How do you explain the living room?

They introduced themselves as "Walter B." and "The Collector." This was not a world. Do you understand? I did not belong there.

If "M" is "How To Use A Crime Instrument..." If "N" is "Boredom..."

Because "O" is "The." Because "O" is "Babies." I did not belong there.

According to "The Ledger," "G" is "The Solution Museum." Can you describe for me what you saw there?

I saw Walter B. belonging.

Did he speak to you?

According to the early drafts, he spoke to me.

THE LEDGER

A Inside The Gesundheithaus
B "The New Pastoral"
C Goat Song; Bought For Two Zuzim
D Letters; Yours; Trace
E Walter B.'s Box Of Things To Do
F Draft
G The Solution Museum
H Adorn; Arrest; Desist
I The Collector
J Nervous System; Gas Lamp
K Daybreak
L Redemption Through Labor
M How To Use A Crime Instrument
N Boredom
O The; Babies
P Muscle; Sadness; Assemblage
Q Form Mimics; Disease
R Basin; Exhibition
S Zug
T Consolidation; Experiment; Lasted
U Tsim Tsum
V Human; Being
W Evidence; Zwang
X Suitcase; Eternal Return
Y From The Undressing Room Into The Living Room
Z Them; Beauty

SIX

TRANSYLVANIA, 1919

"It's good to be back," they say, lifting up the trap door and peeking in. It is early. I was not expecting visitors. I slip off my grandfather's dead lap and smile shyly. Holding hands, they tiptoe down the stairs. Like a long dark draft. Like a century. They are wearing my galoshes. They push their thumbs into my cheeks and pinch my wrists. "Isn't this romantic?" they hiss, pointing at my grandfather until his mouth opens. They circle him and pull the dark zippered stitching from his arm. Upstairs, Mama is ashamed. Mama is shouting at us to go home. Her glasses are mended with string…which reminds me: I climb the stairs. My grandfather coming loose in my arms. I climb the stairs to where Mama is sweeping the swallows into her large brown skirt. She is very old. I kiss my grandfather and gently place him down. As Mama once had. When I first met her. Among the gravel and the circus trailers.

A KADDISH

When Eugene was taken away, the hunter drew the sawdust girl to his chest, and the forest was cold, and they stuffed their mouths with wings until they could feel the raven between them. And when they found Eugene's teeth in their pockets they tried not to smile. It was November. The gods were carefully bathing each other. I combed my hair in the frost. A torn suit fell from a branch, and I laid down next to it. Everywhere the smell of pine. I listened for Eugene, but all I could hear was the hunter lifting the sawdust girl like a veil. All I could hear was shiver, *shiva, shhhs....* The forest was cold. The gods were quietly touching each other in the last black carriage.

THE BLACK UMBRELLA

If love is a girl named Obscure asleep in her black umbrella, then God is among us, and I will happily perform for you my tin-roof tricks. He said, ignore the bamboozle in the lilac, and I did. I broke the bracelet tenderly. I reached in. He said, would you like to see my pocket knife, it's like a little war. He said, a starving octopus has been known to eat her own heart. Have you ever been the only one looking? Have you ever been the only one standing over a black umbrella thinking if you stared hard enough, if you spoke to it…? I heard myself. I thought it was empty. No, I was too afraid to wake it.

Airborne

The plane had no place to land. When the farmer with wet pockets and a prosthetic tongue threatened to call the police I never knew such silence. My name is Oskar. I have a scratch on my thigh. Maybe this is hopeless. Maybe I will wake one day and in your place a bag of black rocks. The lord giveth and the lord...The river tastes like birds today. The plane had no place to land. The farmer was a Jew and lived inside that crushed wall. I have forgotten everything. Looking back over my shoulder, I thought it was a cemetery. I thought it was your charred glove. I walk with a horse's head in my arms. When the lord called war a summer of porn I punched him in the gut. My name is Oskar. I live in that plane. Maybe the rake is hopeless, and the earth is hopeless too. I don't know if I want them back. I am uninhabited. My name is Oskar. I am the sleeve. You are the one armed girl.

THE LIE

The morning after I find the mustache in mother's purse, Brunibar comes to see me. He wants to borrow the mustache, he explains, for the war. I want to ask him how he knows, but I do not dare. I wrap the mustache in a dark blue cloth, along with slices of fish and boiled milk. Our knees touch. We listen to the accordion players kiss the backs of each other's necks on the radio. Brunibar strokes the raised letters on my wrist, and the pockets of my apron grow large. I carry him into mother's bedroom, where a live soldier is chewing a hole through the wall. Brunibar unscrews his wooden foot, and I gently climb inside. "What do you see?" asks Brunibar. "Tents!" I shout, through the black socket. In the distance, mother is already returning from the front. How do I tell Brunibar the truth without hurting him? "Beautiful flying tents," I whisper. My voice growing farther and farther away.

Also Available from **saturnalia books**:

Blackboards

by Tomaž Šalamun and Metka Krašovec

SATURNALIA BOOKS ARTIST/POET COLLABORATION SERIES NO. 1

Apprehend by Elizabeth Robinson
Father of Noise by Anthony McCann
Nota by Martin Corless-Smith
The Red Bird by Joyelle McSweeney
Can You Relax in My House by Michael Earl Craig

The Babies is the winner of the first Saturnalia Books Poetry Prize.

The Babies was printed using the fonts Burlington and Perpetua.